IN THE
NATIONAL INTEREST

General Sir John Monash once exhorted a graduating class to 'equip yourself for life, not solely for your own benefit but for the benefit of the whole community'. At the university established in his name, we repeat this statement to our own graduating classes, to acknowledge how important it is that common or public good flows from education.

Universities spread and build on the knowledge they acquire through scholarship in many ways, well beyond the transmission of this learning through education. It is a necessary part of a university's role to debate its findings, not only with other researchers and scholars, but also with the broader community in which it resides.

Publishing for the benefit of society is an important part of a university's commitment to free intellectual inquiry. A university provides civil space for such inquiry by its scholars, as well as for investigations by public intellectuals and expert practitioners.

This series, In the National Interest, embodies Monash University's mission to extend knowledge and encourage informed debate about matters of great significance to Australia's future.

Professor Sharon Pickering
President and Vice-Chancellor,
Monash University

MATTHEW HARDING

CHARITIES & POLITICS: A PRINCIPLED APPROACH

MONASH
UNIVERSITY
PUBLISHING

Charities & Politics: A Principled Approach
© Copyright 2024 Matthew Harding
All rights reserved. Apart from any uses permitted by Australia's *Copyright Act
1968*, no part of this book may be reproduced by any process without prior
written permission from the copyright owners. Inquiries should be directed
to the publisher.

Monash University Publishing
Matheson Library Annexe
40 Exhibition Walk
Monash University
Clayton, Victoria 3800, Australia
https://publishing.monash.edu

Monash University Publishing brings to the world publications which
advance the best traditions of humane and enlightened thought.

ISBN: 9781923192003 (paperback)
ISBN: 9781923192027 (ebook)

Series: In the National Interest
Editor: Greg Bain
Project manager & copyeditor: Paul Smitz
Designer: Peter Long
Typesetter: Cannon Typesetting
Proofreader: Gillian Armitage
Printed in Australia by Ligare Book Printers

A catalogue record for this book is available from the National Library
of Australia.

The paper this book is printed on is in accordance with the standards of the
Forest Stewardship Council®. The FSC® promotes environmentally responsible,
socially beneficial and economically viable management of the world's forests.

To Clare, Isabel and Charlie.

CHARITIES & POLITICS: A PRINCIPLED APPROACH

This book is about the civil society organisations that are recognised in Australian law as charities. Charities constitute only a minority of the civil society sector in Australia, numbering approximately 60 000 out of an estimated 600 000 organisations formed on a not-for-profit basis and serving the community in one way or another. But while charities are relatively few in number, they play an outsize role in the social, cultural and economic life of the nation. Charities employ more than 10 per cent of Australia's workforce. They generate revenue from a range of sources—including government contracts and grants, fee-for-service income, and philanthropy—of nearly $200 billion annually. They deliver services and provide goods to the public on which lives depend. Charities matter. And so, too, does the law and policy framework in which they operate.

Charity status is prized in civil society. Being recognised in law as a charity subjects an organisation to a regulatory regime administered by Australia's national charity regulator, the Australian Charities and Not-for-profits Commission (ACNC). But it also opens the door to legal privileges, such as an exemption from income tax. Being recognised as a charity has further, less formal but equally important consequences for an organisation, such as eligibility for funding opportunities that are only available to charities, and the reputational benefits that come from being endorsed by the state. So civil society organisations that have a chance of being recognised as a charity usually seek to acquire and maintain that status.

If there ever was a time when charities confined themselves to delivering 'on the ground' goods and services to the community, it is certainly no longer the case today. As much as any other organisation, charities must operate within, and respond to the complexity of, a modern market economy, the demands and expectations of the bureaucratic state, and the needs and interests of a diverse and dynamic polity. Thus, charities increasingly engage in commercial activities, become enmeshed in government structures and priorities, and adopt governance and management models developed in the business and bureaucratic worlds.

They also participate in politics. This takes various forms, including campaigning for changes to law and government policy, challenging the decisions of government officials, and seeking to influence public opinion on issues that are subject to political debate in the public sphere. Charities participate in politics in these ways because they perceive such participation to be the most effective way of doing good for the communities that they serve. They are also expected to engage in these various forms of political advocacy, not only by their communities but also by government itself, which often calls for charity participation in law and policy reform processes.

Notwithstanding that charities engage in political advocacy in a range of important and valued ways, the legal position they face has long been a challenging one, potentially carrying the risk of losing their charity status and associated legal privileges. To see why, it is necessary to step back from the political arena and consider the law that constitutes and regulates charities.

THE OLD *BOWMAN* RULE

The law in question is venerable, dating back to Elizabethan England.[1] Under it, organisations that wish to be accepted legally as charities must be formed for the pursuit of purposes that are recognised in law as charitable and for the public benefit. These purposes have been worked out from case to case by judges over hundreds of years. More recently, in a number of countries, charitable purpose types have been spelt out in legislation, building on those hundreds of years of judge-made law. In Australia, for the purposes of federal law, charitable purpose types are stipulated in section 12 of the *Commonwealth Charities Act* of 2013, ranging from the provision of social welfare to the advancement of education and religion, and the promotion of arts and culture. For the purposes of state law, the judge-made law continues to apply, but there is a high degree of overlap between the charitable purpose types stipulated in the federal charities Act and those developed by the judges in the cases.

Sometimes, an organisation has a purpose that does not fall within one of the types of purpose recognised as charitable in law. In these cases, the organisation must demonstrate that its purpose is for the public benefit, and usually also that its purpose is analogous to a type that is recognised as charitable. And it is here that organisations engaging in political advocacy have fallen foul of the law. Historically, political advocacy was not considered to be a charitable type of purpose. Consequently, organisations engaging in political advocacy had to demonstrate that their purposes were for the public benefit if they were to be recognised in law as charities. But in a series of important decisions, courts, first in England and then elsewhere in the common law world, ruled that political advocacy organisations could not discharge this burden and as a result could not be recognised as charities.

This line of judicial authority is usually thought to begin with remarks made by Lord Parker of Waddington in the 1917 English case of *Bowman v Secular Society*, where it was asserted that

> a trust for the attainment of political objects has always been held invalid, not because it is illegal, for every one is at liberty to advocate or promote by any lawful means a change in the law, but because the Court has no means of judging whether a proposed change in the law will or will not be for the public benefit, and therefore cannot say that a gift to secure the change is a charitable gift.[2]

It is strange that these comments were subsequently treated as an authoritative statement of the law. For one thing, Lord Parker made the remarks in passing, and they did not form part of the reasoning that decided the case. Moreover, contrary to what Lord Parker asserted, it was not true in 1917 that a trust for the attainment of political objects had 'always been held invalid'. Indeed, there is a rich record of charitable organisations undertaking political advocacy in the nineteenth century.[3] Nonetheless, Lord Parker's dicta were endorsed in subsequent cases. Thus, in 1948, the House of Lords ruled that the National Anti-Vivisection Society could not be a charity as its purpose was agitating for law reform in respect of the use of live animals in medical research. And in 1982, in a case involving Amnesty International, Justice Slade of the English High Court of Justice ruled that the purposes of securing the release of prisoners of conscience and procuring the abolition of torture were considered too political to be charitable.

The reasoning of the English courts was adopted elsewhere in the common law world. In New Zealand, for example, the approach from *Bowman v Secular Society* was applied in 1981 in *Molloy v Commissioner of State Revenue*, a case about an organisation campaigning against abortion.[4] And in Australia, that approach was applied as early as the 1930s, although the great Sir Owen Dixon remarked in the case of *Royal North Shore Hospital of Sydney v Attorney-General* that 'the case law dealing with the distinction between charitable purposes and political objects is in an unsatisfactory condition'.[5]

By the turn of the twenty-first century, the old *Bowman* rule had come to be embedded in the charity law of Australia. In light of it, organisations engaging in political advocacy risked being denied charity status, and charities focusing their energies on political advocacy risked losing that status and the legal privileges associated with it. It must be noted that the *Bowman* rule only ever applied to organisations whose constituent purpose was political advocacy. In theory, then, the rule did not affect organisations that engaged in political advocacy as a means to achieve other, charitable, purposes. For example, under the rule, a charity formed for the relief of poverty was always free to advocate on issues affecting the poor. Nonetheless, the persistence of the *Bowman* rule undeniably had a chilling effect on organisations that sought to engage in political advocacy. And this was compounded by the legal uncertainty surrounding the question of how to distinguish between an organisation's constituent purpose on the one hand, and activities supporting that purpose on the other.

The chilling effect was also exacerbated by the prospect that executive government might use the *Bowman* rule to put pressure on charities speaking out in unwelcome ways. In the latter part of the twentieth century, this prospect grew more acute. During that time, governments in liberal democracies around the world retreated from the direct provision of services to the public, preferring instead to fund charities and others to provide those services. On the back of increased government funding, large charities began to professionalise and adopt more sophisticated strategies to achieve public benefit outcomes. These strategies included political advocacy in areas where charities felt government was not doing enough to solve social problems. But for government, there was a growing sense that where charities relied on government funding, they should align with government policies in their areas of operation. At the same time, a range of social trends—including the use of the internet for communication purposes, increasing diversity in religious and other world views, and even political polarisation—saw charities speaking out more on politically contested issues, and in ways that were apt to embarrass government.

This brings us to the landmark 2010 case that effected a substantial change in the Australian approach to charities and politics.

A LEGAL SEA CHANGE

The case was *Aid/Watch Inc v Federal Commissioner of Taxation*. Aid/Watch is an avowedly activist organisation that seeks to bring about political change in respect of Australia's foreign aid and trade programs. It was formed in 1993, and seven years later, the Australian Taxation Office (ATO) endorsed Aid/Watch as a 'charitable institution' for income tax purposes, based on the fact that Aid/Watch's constitution enumerated charitable purposes. This was followed in 2005 by endorsements for fringe benefits tax and goods and services tax purposes. At this time, Aid/Watch was recognised for the purposes of Australia's federal tax law as a charitable organisation notwithstanding its political advocacy orientation.

In October 2006, the federal commissioner of taxation, Michael D'Ascenzo, revoked Aid/Watch's endorsements. In doing so, the commissioner referred to concerns about three activities that Aid/Watch had engaged in: urging the public to write to the Australian Government to put pressure on the

Burmese Government in respect of human rights violations; delivering an ironic sixtieth birthday cake to the World Bank, a stunt that attracted media attention; and raising concerns about the impacts of the US–Australia Free Trade Agreement. The commissioner indicated that these three activities disclosed an unstated political advocacy purpose, and to that extent Aid/Watch was on the wrong side of the *Bowman* rule, notwithstanding the charitable objectives spelled out in its constitution. Aid/Watch challenged the commissioner's notice of revocation and the matter progressed all the way to the High Court.

Why, in 2006, did the commissioner choose to focus on Aid/Watch's activities? In an article published in 2011, James Goodman, an academic who was also one of the founders of Aid/Watch, gave an 'inside' account. Goodman described the political context in 2006 as one in which 'the Australian aid program had become increasingly politicised, and tensions between Aid/Watch and the government had sharpened'.[6] He recounted how then foreign minister Alexander Downer telephoned Aid/Watch's offices threatening to defund the organisation. He noted that the ATO could provide no satisfactory reason for singling out Aid/Watch from the 48 000 tax-exempt charities at that time, and he suggested that members of the government improperly pressured the ATO to investigate Aid/Watch as well as other advocacy organisations endorsed for federal tax purposes. Goodman's account suggests that the prospect of executive government using the *Bowman* rule to stifle dissent from charities was far from a remote one back in 2006.

When Aid/Watch appealed to the Administrative Appeals Tribunal (AAT) against the taxation commissioner's notice of revocation, Justice Downes found for Aid/Watch, stating that the organisation's purposes were charitable and that its advocacy did not disclose some freestanding political purpose. In a sign of what was to come in the High Court of Australia, Justice Downes also voiced concerns with the *Bowman* rule and questioned whether it continued to be appropriate in light of contemporary governmental practices such as consultation on matters of policy and freedom of information. Nonetheless, the full Federal Court overturned Justice Downes's decision, stating it was bound by the *Bowman* rule. Moreover, the court said the rule was justified as it shields judges from having to ascertain the public benefit of political change, a task that judges are neither equipped nor authorised to perform. In the case of Aid/Watch itself, the court said it would not be possible or appropriate for judges to weigh up the various factors bearing on the design of Australia's foreign aid program, in trying to arrive at a finding on the key question of public benefit.

As Goodman later recounted, Aid/Watch very nearly did not appeal the matter to the High Court. However, mindful of the legal significance of the case, the ATO made test-case funding available and this allowed the appeal to go ahead. And in the High Court, the case took an interesting turn. Transcripts of the oral argument indicate that some of the judges were interested not only in the *Bowman* rule itself, but also in the constitutional setting in which the rule operates. For those judges, the pertinent aspect of that constitutional setting was the system of representative and responsible government for which Australia's Constitution provides. In cases dating back to the 1990s, the High Court had extrapolated from this system of representative and responsible government an implied constitutional freedom of political communication—one of the few constitutionally entrenched rights protections that Australians enjoy.

In the *Aid/Watch* case, a majority of the High Court took this reasoning further: if Australia's Constitution provides for a system of representative and responsible government, and if free political communication between electors, government and the legislature is an 'indispensable incident' of that system,[7] then Australia's Constitution recognises that public benefit inheres in free political communication. As Chief Justice French and Justices Gummow, Hayne, Crennan and Bell put it in a key passage of their judgment:

> The system of law which applies in Australia thus postulates for its operation the very 'agitation' for legislative and political changes of which Dixon J spoke in Royal North Shore Hospital … [I]t is the operation of these constitutional processes which contributes to the public welfare.[8]

On this view, for charity law to contain a rule denying the public benefit of free political communication is for the legal system under the Constitution to lack coherence.

The reasoning of the majority in *Aid/Watch* is significant in that it locates the public benefit of political advocacy not in an assessment of the consequences that might flow from the achievement of the ends advocated for, but rather in an assessment of the process benefits attaching to advocacy itself.

The reasoning thus sidesteps the concern expressed by Lord Parker in *Bowman*, and underscored by the full Federal Court in *Aid/Watch*, that judges cannot and should not ascertain the public benefit associated with political change. As the majority in *Aid/Watch* put the matter:

> A court administering a charitable trust … is not called upon to adjudicate the merits of any particular course of legislative or executive action or inaction which is the subject of advocacy or disputation within those processes.[9]

This recognition of the process benefits of political advocacy represents a departure not only from the *Bowman* rule but also from the orthodox approach to applying charity law's public benefit test. Under that approach, the whole constellation of consequences, both good and bad, that might flow from the achievement of a purpose are to be taken into consideration when making an overall assessment of whether public benefit is present on the facts of the case. The majority in *Aid/Watch* appear to suggest that, in cases of political advocacy, some relevant consequences—that is to say, those that relate to the achievement of the ends advocated for—need not be considered. As we will see later, this approach to assessing the public benefit of political advocacy runs into difficulty once the question of the limits of that public benefit is brought into view.

The High Court's reasoning in *Aid/Watch* has had significant implications for Australian charities. But before addressing those, it is worth pausing to consider the views of the two High Court judges who dissented in *Aid/Watch* and would have upheld the decision of the full Federal Court. In order to understand the dissenting judgments, it is necessary to appreciate that the majority in *Aid/Watch* characterised Aid/Watch's constituent purpose as the 'generation by lawful means of public debate ... concerning the efficiency of foreign aid'.[10] The dissenting judges disagreed with this characterisation. In a typically caustic judgment, Justice Heydon stated:

> The appellant [Aid/Watch] advanced points of view, but it was not generating debate in the sense of stimulating others to contribute competing points of view so that some higher synthesis or more acute understanding of issues might emerge. The appellant was not playing the role of a teacher in charge of a skilfully conducted seminar, or someone deftly presiding over a meeting. The appellant's

activities were designed to ensure that the appellant's points of view about aid prevailed by ensuring that government did some things and did not do others ... Those who ran the appellant did not see themselves as philosophers merely talking about the world, or encouraging others to talk about the world: they saw their task as being to change the world ... The appellant's views were not put in a manner inviting a response, but in a manner seeking compliance. It did not want dialogue, nor even too long a monologue. The appellant wanted its views to be implemented, not debated. It wanted obedience, not conversation.[11]

For Justice Heydon, Aid/Watch's purpose of forcing adherence to its views was not charitable and there was no need to investigate the limits of the *Bowman* rule given the facts of the case.

Justice Kiefel also rejected a characterisation of Aid/Watch's constituent purpose as generating public debate about foreign aid delivery. Generating public debate might be educational in character, in which case it is a charitable purpose of public benefit. But in the case of Aid/Watch itself, Justice Kiefel thought that the constituent purpose was the assertion of views about foreign aid delivery. The question of public benefit thus demanded some assessment of the merits of those views, and Justice Kiefel agreed with the full Federal Court that such an assessment was beyond the capability of the courts.

Aid/Watch self-identifies as an activist organisation that seeks to drive change rather than stimulate debate.[12] Given this, the dissenting judges were right to worry about the majority's characterisation of Aid/Watch's constituent purpose. Nonetheless, the significance of the majority's reasoning lies less in their assessment of the facts of the case and more in their articulation of a constitutionally grounded account of the public benefit of political advocacy. It is this account that has generated a sea change in respect of charities and politics in Australian law. Soon after *Aid/Watch* was decided, the majority's reasoning informed the provisions of the federal *Charities Act* of 2013. Under section 12(1)(l) of the Act, political advocacy is expressly recognised as a type of charitable purpose, subject to certain limitations to which we will shortly return. The combination of *Aid/Watch* and section 12(1)(l) has gone a long way to correcting the chilling effect of the old *Bowman* rule, giving charities assurance that political purposes may be charitable at least in certain circumstances.

THE LANDSCAPE AFTER *AID/WATCH*

Aid/Watch provided needed clarity on the question of whether political advocacy can be a charitable purpose for the public benefit. Nonetheless, the reasoning of the majority in that case left some important questions unresolved. One such question is whether public benefit is present only where a charity's political advocacy relates to a recognised charitable purpose type. If public benefit is present only in those circumstances, then an organisation with the purpose of engaging in political advocacy to pressure government to act on poverty could be considered a charity of public benefit, but an organisation with the purpose of, say, advocating for a new approach to Australia's diplomatic relations with the United States could not. This is because the relief of poverty is an accepted type of charitable purpose in Australian law, while furthering Australia's diplomatic relations with foreign countries is not.

On the one hand, the reasoning of the majority in *Aid/Watch* highlighted process benefits that attend political advocacy in general. On the other hand, the majority decided in favour of Aid/Watch on the basis that generating public debate about matters relating to recognised charitable purposes is for the public benefit. For the purposes of federal law, the uncertainty has been resolved in the *Charities Act 2013*. Section 12 makes clear that political advocacy is a charitable purpose for the public benefit only where it relates to one of the charitable purpose types enumerated in that section. Nonetheless, as a matter of principle, it must be asked whether such a limitation on recognising political advocacy as a charitable purpose is arbitrary.

A further unresolved question, which arose upon the enactment of the *Charities Act*, goes to the interaction of the majority's reasoning in *Aid/Watch* with section 6 of that Act. Section 6 is addressed to a decision-maker who is tasked with assessing whether an organisation's constituent purpose is of public benefit. Such a decision-maker is required to have regard to 'all relevant matters', which include 'benefits (whether tangible or intangible)' and 'any possible, identifiable detriment from the achievement of the purpose'. In a case where a decision-maker is required to assess whether a political advocacy purpose is of public benefit, section 6 appears to require consideration not only of process benefits attaching to political advocacy itself, but also benefits and detriments associated with the achievement of the end advocated for. This does not sit easily with the majority's reasoning in *Aid/Watch*, which seems to suggest that such an assessment of benefits and detriments associated with ends might not be required.

Then there is the question of political parties. These have never been regarded as charities for the public benefit, even though they engage in free political communication in exactly the way that the Australian Constitution implies is of public benefit. When *Aid/Watch* was before the High Court, Justice Gummow tested counsel on the reasons why political parties and partisan purposes are not regarded as charitable under Australian law.[13] However, the questions he raised were not addressed in the judgments in the case. Since the enactment of the *Charities Act*, the legal position has been clear-cut: section 11 states that 'the purpose of promoting or opposing a political party or a candidate for political office' cannot be charitable under the Act, before going on to explain that the rule 'does not apply to the purpose of distributing information, or advancing debate, about the policies of political parties or candidates for political office (such as by assessing, critiquing, comparing or ranking those policies)'. But while the legal position is clear, and organisations know what they can and cannot do consistent with charity status, the question of principle remains. If there are process benefits associated with political advocacy, then why are these never sufficient to ground a finding of public benefit in the case of a political party or a partisan purpose? We will return to this question later on.

UNDER PRESSURE

Aid/Watch may have helped to alleviate the chilling effect of the old *Bowman* rule on charities that engage in political advocacy. But it did not solve the underlying problem of executive government putting pressure on such charities. Indeed, in the years since the High Court's decision, politically engaged charities have been subjected to a range of measures designed to thwart or suppress their advocacy work. For example, in 2014 the Abbott government introduced 'gag' clauses into funding agreements for community legal centres, designed to restrict the extent to which recipients of government funding could speak up against government policy and advocate for law reform—these clauses had been used widely by the Howard government before being abandoned under the Gillard government in 2013. In 2022, the Albanese government removed the 2014 gag clauses, leaving community legal centres free to engage in advocacy on matters of law and policy.

So for the moment, then, charities have the assurance that the federal government has set its face against such clauses. But of course, a future government might feel differently, in which case gag clauses could be revived once again.

Another post-*Aid/Watch* development was the 2016 inquiry into the Register of Environmental Organisations (REO). Environmental organisations that wished to be endorsed by the ATO as able to receive tax-deductible gifts to support their work were required to appear on the REO, which was administered by the Commonwealth Department of the Environment. The terms of reference for the inquiry, overseen by the House of Representatives Standing Committee on the Environment, focused on the 'administration and transparency' of the REO and its effectiveness in 'supporting communities to take practical action to improve the environment'. The reference to 'practical action' indicated a political motivation for the inquiry that was of great concern to advocacy charities, as it suggested a distinction between environmental organisations delivering 'on the ground' benefits and those advocating for environmental causes. And indeed, on the conclusion of the inquiry, a majority of the committee recommended changes to the tax law to require organisations on the

REO to spend no less than 25 per cent of their income on 'environmental remediation work'.

Liberal MP Jason Wood and the Labor members of the committee were moved to write separate reports arguing against the recommendation, with the Labor members stating that

> [we] find it extraordinary that government members have recommended to, in effect, constrain the capacity of environmental organisations to engage in advocacy work. We completely reject this undemocratic proposition. Citizens should be supported to question government decision-making and corporate power, not manoeuvred into silence by legislative and administrative action.[14]

The recommendation was never implemented, and the REO ceased to exist on 1 January 2024 thanks to other recommendations of the inquiry, but the threat to environmental advocacy charities was a real one nonetheless.

The years of conservative government under prime ministers Abbott, Turnbull and Morrison continued in various ways to be challenging ones for advocacy charities. In 2017, Gary Johns was appointed commissioner of the Australian Charities and Not-for-profits Commission, replacing inaugural commissioner Susan Pascoe. The ACNC had been established by the Gillard government in 2012, and it had been welcomed by the charity sector as a long overdue and much needed development. Nonetheless, Johns's appointment as commissioner caused disquiet in the sector. He was perceived as hostile to charities, and especially to charities engaging in political advocacy, and many in the sector expected him to mount test cases challenging *Aid/Watch* and putting under threat the jurisprudential gains that the case had brought about. The chilling effect was back.

On the legislative front, in 2017 the Turnbull government proposed changes to federal electoral law, ostensibly to reduce and control foreign interference in Australian elections. This was a worthy aim, but the legislation was drafted in such a way that it would have required charities engaging in political advocacy to disclose and manage huge numbers of donations upon threat of sanction.[15] The changes were not made in the form proposed, and the threat abated. But at the end of 2021, the threat returned. The Morrison government successfully steered legislation through parliament requiring a range of advocacy charities to register as political campaigners for the purposes of electoral law. This placed the charities concerned under onerous reporting requirements, especially in relation to their donors.[16] The full effects of the legislative changes will be felt across the Australian charity sector in the years to come.

For the charity sector, 2021 was a dangerous year in another respect. At the same time as the proposed changes to the electoral law were being debated, the Morrison government sought to introduce changes to the 'governance standards' to which most ACNC-registered charities are subject.[17] These changes would have placed a charity at risk of deregistration or other regulatory action in circumstances where its political advocacy activity entailed even minor, inadvertent breaches of law—a real possibility for a charity engaged in or supporting protest activity. Advocacy charities did not dispute that they should be subject to law and face appropriate sanctions for breaches. However, they viewed the prospect of deregistration for minor, advertent breaches as disproportionate, and they argued that the proposed changes to the governance standards were designed to stifle and silence charities that sought to speak out on issues of the day.

The changes were blocked in the Senate and never came to pass.[18] For the charity sector, this was a significant win at a time when it was widely felt that the government was determined to stop advocacy charities from doing their work.

SOME WELCOME CLARITY?

This somewhat dismal account of the post-*Aid/Watch* years reveals that the High Court's decision did not solve the problem of executive government seeking to make life difficult for advocacy charities. But we should not lose sight of what the decision did achieve. It laid to rest, possibly once and for all, the notion that political advocacy cannot be a charitable purpose of public benefit. And in doing that, the decision made it more difficult than it had previously been for executive government to threaten advocacy charities with the loss of their charity status. Thus, the record of post-*Aid/Watch* efforts to rein in charity advocacy is a record of reaching for indirect means—electoral law, regulatory practice and so forth—to do so.

In July 2024, the federal assistant minister responsible for the charity sector, Andrew Leigh, delivered an important speech to the Charity Law Association of Australia and New Zealand annual conference in Wellington. Leigh gave sector representatives assurance that the current federal government is not disposed to stifle or interfere with charity advocacy:

In Opposition, Labor joined the sector to oppose a series of challenges to the charity sector's right and ability to advocate for their purpose. In government, we continue to celebrate the important role of nongovernment voices in policy development and public discourse.[19]

Leigh went on to indicate that he has promised to consider a draft Bill prepared by the Stronger Charities Alliance, a group that promotes charity advocacy. The draft Bill, if adopted by the federal government, would be a landmark recognition and protection of the public benefit associated with charity advocacy, taking its place alongside the ruling in *Aid/Watch* and section 12(l) of the *Charities Act 2013*. Whether anything will come of Leigh's promise remains to be seen.

The sea change brought about by *Aid/Watch* has opened up new frontiers for jurisprudential debate in respect of advocacy charities. The question of whether political advocacy can be a charitable purpose of public benefit has been resolved in Australian law. Attention has now turned to a different question with equally important ramifications for advocacy charities. In Australian law, being recognised as a charity opens the door to certain tax privileges.

In federal law, the key one is income tax exemption. In state law, the privileges include payroll tax exemption and exemption from land taxes. The availability of these tax privileges is one reason why charity status is highly prized by civil society organisations, and why executive government polices the boundaries of charity so jealously.

That said, one of the most desired tax privileges on offer to civil society organisations under Australian law is not available to all charities. This is the privilege of being able to attract tax-deductible gifts from donors. In order to enjoy this privilege, a charity must meet additional criteria, and the law spelling these out is complex. For present purposes, it will suffice to notice that a charity may attract tax-deductible gifts from donors if, in addition to being a charity, it is also registered by the ACNC commissioner as a 'public benevolent institution' within the meaning of division 30 of Australia's *Income Tax Assessment Act 1997*. It is in respect of this category—'public benevolent institution'—that jurisprudential debate has opened up about advocacy charities post-*Aid/Watch*.

Under what circumstances can an advocacy charity be described as a 'public benevolent institution' as that term is understood in Australian law?

The answer to this question determines whether advocacy charities can attract tax-deductible gifts, and thus affects their fundraising capacity in significant ways. In a series of recent cases, Australian courts and tribunals have begun to shed light on the question in ways that suggest it might not be long before it receives an authoritative answer to guide future law and practice.

In 2014, the full Federal Court had to consider whether an organisation called The Hunger Project was a 'public benevolent institution'.[20] The Hunger Project was formed for the relief of poverty and suffering, especially in the developing world. However, it did not deliver aid to the needy directly. Rather, it raised funds that it then distributed to associated organisations globally, and those organisations spent those distributed funds in delivering aid. The Federal Court found that, in order to be 'benevolent', an organisation need not alleviate poverty and suffering directly. It is sufficient that the organisation does so indirectly, in this case through raising and distributing funds. This ruling is significant for advocacy charities seeking status as 'public benevolent institutions', as their advocacy might often be regarded as supporting good outcomes for needy people only indirectly.

The jurisprudence was further developed by the AAT in the 2021 case of *Global Citizen Ltd v Commissioner of the Australian Charities and Not-for-profits Commission*. Global Citizen is an organisation dedicated to raising funds from government and philanthropists to support efforts to relieve global poverty. It runs highly effective public events to raise awareness of its mission, including the annual Global Citizen Festival—the 2024 festival was held in Melbourne, and the star-studded line-up of participants included East Timor Prime Minister Xanana Gusmão, Julia Gillard and the Duchess of York. In 2018, Global Citizen sought to be registered as a 'public benevolent institution' to attract tax-deductible gifts, but the application was refused by the then ACNC commissioner Gary Johns. In the AAT, deputy president Bernard McCabe and senior member Ann O'Connell relied on the decision of the full Federal Court in the case about The Hunger Project, pointing out that Australian law recognises benevolence that is indirect. For the AAT, Global Citizen's fundraising and awareness-raising activities, while indirect, were sufficiently related to the objective of ending global poverty to render the organisation 'benevolent' in the sense required by the law.

This was captured nicely in a witness statement by the Reverend Tim Costello, a supporter of Global Citizen: 'I believe advocacy, awareness raising and/or education of the type that Global Citizen undertakes does relieve poverty.'[21]

In *Global Citizen*, then, the AAT confirmed what the Federal Court had said earlier about indirect benevolence, and it did so in finding for an organisation whose activities include political advocacy. However, the AAT also had this to say:

> One of the issues raised in the case was whether advocating for changes in government policy (eg, concerning levels of aid or legislative change relating to gender discrimination) would be concrete enough to amount to relieving poverty. We do not need to decide this matter because it is clear the activities of [Global Citizen] go beyond mere advocacy for policy change.[22]

This, of course, is the critical question for advocacy charities seeking recognition as 'public benevolent institutions'. At the time of writing, there is a live case that may resolve it authoritatively. The case relates to the charity Equality Australia, which was first formed in 2015 under the name Australians for Equality.

Its purpose at that time was to advocate for marriage equality, a goal that was famously realised following the same-sex marriage referendum in 2017. In 2018, the charity revisited the question of its purpose and reoriented itself to campaign and advocate on discrimination in religious settings, gender identity and conversion therapy, among other issues. It was at this time that it rebranded itself Equality Australia. However, while Equality Australia's raison d'être might have changed over time, its character as an advocacy charity remained, and remains, the same.

In 2020, Equality Australia applied to be registered as a 'public benevolent institution', but this application was rejected by Johns. The matter then proceeded to the AAT, where McCabe and O'Connell were once again sitting, this time alongside member Louise Bygrave. There were two questions for the AAT to determine. The first was whether the LGBTIQ+ community whose interests are served by Equality Australia can be considered in need of benevolence. The second was the question raised but not answered in *Global Citizen*: whether an organisation can be 'benevolent' if it seeks to improve the circumstances of those who are suffering through political advocacy. The three members of the AAT all agreed that members of the LGBTIQ+ community could be thought in need of benevolence. To some minds, this might suggest a paternalism towards a community that seeks change through empowerment, but that is a matter for another day. On the second question, the AAT were split. McCabe and Bygrave stated that there must be a sufficiency of connection between an organisation's activities and the relief of suffering that it seeks to bring about. Indirect benevolence is permitted, so long as it is not *too* indirect. And for these two members, Equality Australia had not demonstrated the sufficiency of connection that is required. On the other hand, O'Connell considered that Equality Australia's advocacy was part of a broader range of activities. including education and support. Viewed in this setting, Equality Australia, like Global Citizen, had demonstrated a sufficient connection between its methods and the relief of suffering.

The Equality Australia case is currently before the full Federal Court. Many are hoping that the court will clarify the legal position on the key question raised in *Global Citizen*, which to some extent remains unanswered. Can an advocacy charity be a public benevolent institution? Or must the charity carry out other work in the nature of education and support? But a word of caution is in order. In thinking about the prospect of the court delivering the desired clarity, it is worth reflecting carefully on this passage from the reasons of Ann O'Connell in the case:

> A characterisation process which does not set out express criteria invites the decision-maker to stand back, review the stated purpose and activities of the organisation, and make a broad evaluative judgment as to that organisation's essential nature. The evaluation must be objective, and it must be evidence-based, but it ultimately involves forming an impression. It is not a question that can be resolved through exact proof: as courts have observed in other contexts, sometimes, one just knows whether something meets a definition when one sees it. The best a decision-maker can do is describe the basis of the impression. While that might strike some as being unsatisfactorily vague, it is almost certainly what parliament intended in this case when it used a multi-faceted word like 'benevolent'.[23]

That, with respect, seems undeniable.

To sum up, then, the landscape after *Aid/Watch* is one in which there is welcome clarity on the fundamental question that dogged charity law for decades. Political advocacy can be a charitable purpose of public benefit. At the same time, though, some key questions remain unanswered about the outer limits of that proposition; for example, in relation to political parties and partisan purposes. Executive government has lost a weapon with which to thwart and silence charities that speak out, but the post-*Aid/Watch* record shows there are plenty of other weapons in the arsenal, and advocacy charities must remain vigilant. Finally, the jurisprudential clarification in *Aid/Watch* has shifted the theatre of debate to a further set of questions, about whether advocacy charities can be 'public benevolent institutions' and thereby attract tax-deductible gifts. There may well be further sea changes to come.

INTERNATIONAL COMPARISONS

We saw earlier that the *Bowman* rule, stating that political advocacy cannot be a charitable purpose for the public benefit, was adopted throughout the common law world following its acceptance in England. In some of the jurisdictions where this has occurred, there have been interesting recent developments both in relation to the rule itself and, more broadly, in relation to charity advocacy. I want to focus on three such jurisdictions: England and Wales, Canada, and New Zealand. In each of these, just as in Australia, questions have been raised recently about restrictions on charity advocacy. But in none of the jurisdictions have those questions received unproblematic answers.

Consider England and Wales. In 2012, the Charity Commission of England and Wales denied charitable status to an organisation called the Human Dignity Trust (HDT). HDT campaigns to end the criminalisation of consensual sexual relations in countries where such relations continue to be outlawed. Backed by an array of luminaries from the legal, political and business worlds, HDT has played an active role in supporting strategic human rights litigation to overturn discriminatory laws around the world; for example, HDT recently supported an LGBTIQ+ activist who successfully challenged the constitutionality of 'sodomy' and 'unnatural offences' laws in Namibia.[24] HDT appealed against the decision of the Charity Commission not to register it, and the matter was determined by a tribunal that reviews decisions of the Charity Commission. The tribunal noted that the *Bowman* rule continues to apply in English law, so that an organisation whose constituent purpose is campaigning to change the law cannot be a charity. However, the tribunal went on to say that in its view, HDT was not such an organisation and it ordered the Charity Commission to register HDT as a charity.

The key to the tribunal's reasoning was the fact that the strategic litigation in which HDT engages seeks to impugn the criminal laws of particular countries in light of those countries' constitutional and international law commitments. To that extent, HDT is not so much trying to change the law as it is trying to enforce constitutional and international law. In a key passage of their reasons, the tribunal had this to say:

> We are not satisfied that the litigation supported and conducted by HDT may be described as seeking to change the law. It seems to us that the constitutional process involved in interpreting and/or enforcing superior constitutional rights might, on one analysis, be seen as upholding the law of the state concerned rather than changing it, but it also seems to us that the paradigm of changing/upholding the law is one more suited to an analysis of domestic provisions than it is to the arena of constitutional rights. We prefer to characterise HDT's activities as engaging in a legitimate constitutional process which occupies a different space from that occupied by the domestic law, although we accept that the

outcome of that process may have implications for the domestic law.[25]

In short, the tribunal drew what it thought was a significant distinction between campaigning to have legislation repealed through ordinary political processes, and seeking to have legislation invalidated through human rights litigation.

Does this distinction stand up to scrutiny? After all, in each case the purpose is the same: campaigning against the legislation in question. It seems arguable that whether the campaigning entails engagement in political processes or mounting litigation is irrelevant to whether the campaigning is political in the way that activates the *Bowman* rule. None of this is to say that the *Bowman* rule is justified or desirable or should have been applied against HDT. It is, rather, to say that a political purpose is no less political simply because the method by which it is pursued is the conduct of strategic human rights litigation.

On the other hand, holding a country to its constitutional and international law commitments might best be characterised as seeking to uphold the rule of law, and seeking to uphold the rule of law has long been regarded as a charitable purpose of public benefit. And then there is the possibility that HDT's constituent purpose is simply the promotion of human rights—recognised in section 3(1)(h) of the English and Welsh Charities Act of 2011 as a charitable purpose type—and that conducting strategic human rights litigation is nothing more than a means to the achievement of that charitable end. On this view, HDT's case did not engage the *Bowman* rule at all and so there was no need to discuss whether holding a country to its constitutional and international law commitments falls foul of that rule. Regrettably, these matters were not addressed by the tribunal, and as a result its decision in the HDT case raises as many questions as it answers.

In Canada, matters have taken a different path. The *Bowman* rule applies in that country, as evidenced in the 1998 decision of the Federal Court of Appeal in *Human Life International v Minister of National Revenue*. Human Life International (HLI) campaigns against abortion, and Revenue Canada had registered HLI as a charitable organisation for tax purposes since 1984, but in 1994 this registration was revoked following an extended investigation. The concern appears to have been that HLI moved away from advancing its cause through educational means and began to engage in more provocative tactics. Among other things, the organisation held a public rally and sent members of parliament postcards with graphic images of aborted foetuses. In the Federal Court of Appeal, the *Bowman* rule and its historic rationale were affirmed and adopted:

> [H]ow can we judge which are the views beneficial to society whose distribution merits the name of charity? … Any determination by this Court as to whether the propagation of such views is beneficial to the community and thus worthy of temporal support through tax exemption would be essentially a political determination and is not appropriate for a court to make.[26]

Against this already restrictive backdrop, the Canada Revenue Agency (CRA) imposed a further severe limitation on the extent to which charities could engage in political advocacy. Recall that the *Bowman* rule applies only to organisations whose constituent purpose is political advocacy. The rule has never applied to organisations who engage in advocacy because they think this is the most effective way of achieving their charitable purposes. Nonetheless, Canada's federal Income Tax Act of 1985 contained rules directed at such organisations. According to those rules, a charitable organisation was required to spend 'substantially all' of its resources each year on 'charitable activities' as opposed to 'political activities'. And the CRA issued a policy statement explaining that it understood 'substantially all' in this legislative rule to mean 90 per cent. As a result, Canadian charities could spend only 10 per cent of their annual income on political advocacy if they wanted to be sure of retaining their income tax exemption.

As we have seen, many charities consider political advocacy the most effective way to achieve their charitable purposes. The CRA's position was so at odds with this reality that it was only a matter of time before both the position and the underlying legislative provisions were challenged. Enter Canada Without Poverty, an organisation first formed fifty years ago as the National Anti-Poverty Organisation, and which has a bold mission: to eradicate poverty in Canada. The organisation is clear that it pursues its mission by focusing on public education and—critically for present purposes—on identifying public policy solutions to the problem of poverty. According to Canada Without Poverty's website, 'People don't live in poverty because of poor choices. People live in poverty because of weak policies.'[27] For this organisation, political advocacy is inextricably linked to its underlying charitable purpose.

In 2012, the Canadian Government funded the CRA to undertake audits of organisations that were thought to be engaging in political advocacy critical of government policies. Canada Without Poverty was subject to this scrutiny, and the CRA indicated that it intended to revoke Canada Without Poverty's registration as a tax-exempt charity. Canada Without Poverty then went to court, arguing that the relevant provisions of the Income Tax Act of 1985, as well as the CRA's policy statement, were in violation of the right to freedom of political expression protected by the Canadian Charter of Rights and Freedoms. As was the case in the Australian *Aid/Watch* case, then, a court was invited to consider the constitutional implications of charities engaging in political advocacy.

Justice Morgan, in the Ontario Superior Court of Justice, declared unconstitutional both the relevant provisions of the Income Tax Act and the CRA's policy statement. The judge reasoned that no advocacy organisation has a constitutional right to be recognised as a charity. The state may legitimately refuse to recognise, as charitable, those organisations whose constituent purpose is political advocacy. Thus, the *Bowman* rule is entirely consistent with Canada's constitutional commitments. However, the judge continued, once the state recognises an organisation as a charity, the state cannot then interfere with that organisation's freedom of political expression on pain of losing its charitable status. Having recognised the organisation as charitable, and extended to it an income-tax exemption (and possibly other benefits as well), the state cannot then withdraw that recognition and that support simply because the organisation engages in political expression. To do so would be to act unconstitutionally.

The decision in the 2018 case *Canada Without Poverty v Attorney-General* was significant from a constitutional perspective, because it stood in contrast to the general constitutional position that withholding a subsidy from an advocacy organisation does not constitute an interference with that organisation's speech.[28] It was also a welcome decision as it swept away legislative provisions and government policy that combined to fetter charity advocacy in significant ways. Nonetheless, as was the case in England and Wales in the *Human Dignity Trust* case, the decision of Justice Morgan left key questions unanswered. Why exactly is providing and then withdrawing a subsidy unconstitutional, whereas simply withholding the subsidy in the first place is constitutionally acceptable? And if Canada's constitutional protection of free political expression responds to fundamental political values, then how do those values bear on the *Bowman* rule? This, of course, was the question that troubled a majority of the High Court of Australia in *Aid/Watch*. For the time being, it remains unresolved in Canadian law.

This brings us to New Zealand, a country where advocacy organisations have been before the courts several times in recent years. Three cases are especially worthy of mention. The first involves Greenpeace, which was recognised in New Zealand as a tax-exempt charity until 2010. In that year, the then New Zealand Charity Commission declined to register Greenpeace as a charity under a new scheme established by the country's Charities Act of 2005. Greenpeace appealed that decision and the matter went all the way to New Zealand's apex Supreme Court. In a landmark decision, a majority of the court found that the *Bowman* rule should no longer have any application in New Zealand law. In ruling this way, the majority did not deliberate at any length on the historical justifications for the rule. Instead, they spent some time rejecting the proposition that the New Zealand Parliament had codified the *Bowman* rule in provisions of the Charities Act.

By the time the *Greenpeace* case was before the courts, the High Court of Australia had decided

Aid/Watch. At first instance in the New Zealand High Court, Justice Heath expressed some sympathy with the reasoning of the majority in *Aid/Watch*, to the effect that the public benefit of charity advocacy is to be found in the contribution that advocacy makes to a system of representative and responsible government. Nonetheless, in the New Zealand Court of Appeal, there was little discussion of *Aid/Watch*. And the Supreme Court did not engage with the majority reasoning in *Aid/Watch* either, even though Greenpeace had specifically invited the court to do so. Instead, in *Greenpeace* the majority reasoned that a political advocacy purpose should be subjected to charity law's public benefit test in the same way as other constituent purposes are. What was required was an overall assessment of the benefits and detriments associated with the achievement of the end advocated for, along with the means adopted—advocacy—and the manner in which the advocacy was carried out. This approach differed from that of the majority in *Aid/Watch* to the extent that the *Aid/Watch* majority thought public benefit might be established without having to consider the ends advocated for.

In relation to the end advocated for, the majority in *Greenpeace* was troubled by cases where the end in question is a matter of public controversy. In such a case, the majority thought that it would be difficult for an organisation to demonstrate with evidence that the achievement of the end advocated for would benefit the public. Thus, an organisation campaigning for or against the criminalisation of abortion would have trouble demonstrating public benefit. So would an organisation campaigning for legal supports for voluntary assisted dying. And indeed, the majority thought that *Greenpeace* itself might be such a difficult case. The political end in dispute in *Greenpeace* was the promotion of peace, nuclear disarmament and the elimination of weapons of mass destruction. Would the achievement of this end benefit the New Zealand public? The majority, mindful of domestic and international political factors bearing on the question, expressed scepticism that public benefit could be proven. For one thing, this would require demonstrating that peace is always preferable to war! Nonetheless, the matter was referred back to the successor to the Charity Commission, the Department of Internal Affairs, to be decided in light of the facts and the law.

Perhaps predictably, when the department then considered the matter once again, it declined to register Greenpeace on the basis that public benefit could not be proven. It was only in 2020, when the matter went to the High Court a second time, that an order was finally made to register Greenpeace as a charity. However, the judge who made the order did not form a view on the public benefit of the promotion of peace, nuclear disarmament and the elimination of weapons of mass destruction. Rather, Justice Mallon recharacterised Greenpeace's constituent purpose as advocacy for environmental protection. For Justice Mallon, that end was not controversial in New Zealand and, to that extent, it may be demonstrated readily to be of public benefit. But is this correct? Many would dispute the proposition that advocacy for environmental protection is not a matter of political controversy in New Zealand, raising the possibility that Justice Mallon did not acknowledge the contestable value judgment that she made in deciding the case in the way she did.

In relation to the means and manner adopted in engaging in political advocacy, the majority in *Greenpeace* were vaguer. At one point in their judgment, they made reference to the fact that 'advocacy [for law reform] may well constitute in itself a public good which is analogous to other good works within the sense the law considers charitable'.[29]

Later, in an equally cryptic passage, they stated that

> public benefit or utility may sometimes be found in advocacy or other expressive conduct. But such finding depends on the wider context (including the context of public participation in processes and human rights values), which requires closer consideration than has been brought to bear in the present case.[30]

These passages call to mind the reasoning of the majority of the High Court of Australia in *Aid/Watch*. Nonetheless, they left the question of process benefits associated with charity advocacy largely unexplored.

The 2020 decision of Justice Mallon finally ended Greenpeace's epic battle with the New Zealand Government. The organisation is now registered as a charity for the purposes of New Zealand law. Nonetheless, as was the case with *Aid/Watch* in Australia and *Canada Without Poverty* in Canada, the Supreme Court of New Zealand's decision in *Greenpeace* raised more questions than it answered. How should public benefit be ascertained in cases of political advocacy, especially where the ends advocated for are matters of public controversy?

And to what extent may process benefits of the type recognised in *Aid/Watch* play a role in an overall determination of public benefit based on the ends advocated for, the means adopted, and the manner in which advocacy is carried out?

These questions have been further considered in two subsequent New Zealand cases, one of which, like *Greenpeace*, took a tortured course all the way to the Supreme Court. That case involved an advocacy charity with a very different profile and outlook to that of Greenpeace: Family First New Zealand. Family First's mission is to promote and uphold the traditional family as the central organising unit of New Zealand society. To that end, it undertakes educational, research and advocacy work on a range of issues touching the family, including same-sex marriage, abortion, voluntary assisted dying, the corporal punishment of children, pornography and surrogacy, to name just a few. Family First had been recognised and registered as a charity under New Zealand's Charities Act of 2005. However, in 2013, the Charities Registration Board deregistered the organisation, applying the *Bowman* rule in doing so. In 2014, the Supreme Court of New Zealand handed down its decision in *Greenpeace*, stating that the *Bowman* rule no longer applied in New Zealand law, and so Family First appealed against the deregistration decision on that basis. In the High Court, the deregistration decision was quashed and the matter was referred back to the Charities Registration Board, to be considered again in light of the law laid down in *Greenpeace*.

This the Charities Registration Board duly did, but once again the board refused to register Family First, now on the basis that advocating for the traditional family could not be demonstrated to be for the public benefit given that in New Zealand society, the value of the traditional family is a matter of political controversy. So Family First went again to the High Court. Justice France was happy to state that advocacy for the family, whatever its form, is a public benefit purpose. However, he went on to note that Family First confines its advocacy to the traditional family only. And, for Justice France, this raised problems with respect to public benefit. Family First's advocacy entailed seeking the withdrawal of civil rights from non-traditional families, which could not be said to be of public benefit. The appeal was dismissed.

By now it had been five years since Family First was first deregistered, but the organisation was determined to appeal further. The case proceeded to New Zealand's Court of Appeal, and because of the public interest associated with the case, the Charity Law Association of Australia and New Zealand joined as an intervener. In the Court of Appeal, a majority found in favour of Family First, on the basis that one of its constituent purposes was in fact the advancement of education about the family, and on the basis that its other constituent purpose—advocating for the traditional family—was self-evidently of public benefit notwithstanding that the traditional family is just one kind of family in New Zealand today. The majority also noted an argument raised by the Charity Law Association of Australia and New Zealand, and inspired by *Aid/Watch*, that there are process benefits associated with political advocacy irrespective of the ends advocated for. However, Justice Gilbert wrote a robust dissent, rejecting the proposition that Family First had a constituent purpose to advance education, and insisting that the organisation's raison d'être was to engage in issue advocacy on a range of highly contested social issues. For Justice Gilbert, Family First had not done nearly enough to demonstrate that such issue advocacy was of public benefit.

The Family First case did not end there, though. A further appeal, this time from the attorney-general, as the protector and enforcer of charity under the law, went to the Supreme Court of New Zealand, where a plurality of Chief Justice Winkelmann and Justices Young, Glazebrook and O'Regan ruled that Family First was not formed for the advancement of education, as its promulgation of viewpoints lacked the neutrality and impartiality that is essential to education. On the question of whether promoting the traditional family is of public benefit, the plurality agreed with Justice France that this purpose cannot be said to be self-evidently beneficial to the public as it entails discrimination against non-traditional families. Moreover, the plurality agreed with Justice Gilbert that Family First had a purpose of engaging in issue advocacy on a range of highly contested social issues, and once again could not demonstrate associated public benefit.

In a separate judgment, Justice Williams agreed with the reasons of the plurality and added some highly thought-provoking reflections, to which we will return later:

> [P]romoting controversial causes or ideas will not of itself be disqualifying. This is consistent with authority and (more importantly) the pluralist underpinnings of our democratic culture. As noted in the education context, the contest of ideas and perspectives is a predicate for a thriving community.

But care is obviously needed, and it is perhaps in this context that manner and means, and the original charitable principle of selflessness, become very important. An advocacy group that addresses a controversial topic in a balanced way may well be charitable, even if it ultimately favours one side or the other. Honesty and respect in debate is not self-referential. In fact it can contribute to social cohesion and the empowerment of individuals while respecting also the communicator's right to their point of view. It can assist the community to navigate its way through difficult issues. And there is certainly no shortage of those right now.[31]

With the decision of the Supreme Court, Family First's eight-year battle to regain its charity status was lost. Nonetheless, the organisation continues to operate, underscoring the important point that an organisation can advocate freely and even effectively without being a charity.

The last of the recent New Zealand cases worth noticing relates to the Better Public Media Trust, an organisation that advocates for the provision of strong, impartial public media in New Zealand. It was formed in 2013 following campaigns to save Radio New Zealand from commercialisation and Television

New Zealand Channel 7 from closure. In 2016 it sought registration as a charity and in 2019 its application was rejected by the Charities Registration Board, on the basis that its advocacy for viewpoints relating to public media could not be shown to be of public benefit. On appeal to the New Zealand High Court, the decision of the board was upheld. However, in the Court of Appeal, the Better Public Media Trust won and the board was ordered to register the organisation as a charity. For the Court of Appeal, the Better Public Media Trust's advocacy was self-evidently of public benefit in light of the conditions for a 'free and healthy democracy', which include a vibrant and independent public media sector.[32] In this way, the organisation's advocacy could be distinguished from that of Family First, which could not be so easily reconciled with liberal democratic values.

This excursion into international comparisons has been long and detailed, but it provides important context when considering charities and politics in Australian law. For one thing, the international experience demonstrates that advocacy charities are coming under pressure from executive government all over the world, including in liberal democracies. The events leading up to the *Canada Without Poverty* case illustrate this well. So do the sorry tales of protracted intervention on the part of New Zealand's Charity Commission and Charities Registration Board against Greenpeace, Family First and the Better Public Media Trust. In this respect, the Australian record is far from unique. Moreover, the international experience reveals that courts and tribunals in several countries have struggled to articulate the grounds and limits of public benefit when it comes to political advocacy. This is arguably one reason why cases about advocacy charities continue to occupy the courts, including apex courts such as the High Court of Australia and the Supreme Court of New Zealand.

On the other hand, the cases from Australia, England and Wales, Canada and New Zealand suggest that the right place to search for a principled approach to the question of political advocacy and public benefit is in constitutional commitments and the political and moral values associated with those commitments. That guidance is helpful. But what appears to be lacking in any of the jurisdictions we have traversed is a coherent account that works out from political and moral values to the public benefit of political advocacy, and from there seeks to identify the limits of that public benefit. It is to that task that we now turn.

A PRINCIPLED APPROACH

In seeking a principled approach to the questions raised by charities and politics, we should pause to consider the justifications that judges and others have offered for the old *Bowman* rule. In doing this, we need look no further than *Bowman* itself. There, Lord Parker stated his view that judges called on to work out the public benefit associated with changing the law would have 'no means' available to do so. It is this argument that, until recently, courts around the common law world have pointed to when justifying their adoption and maintenance of the *Bowman* rule.

One point to note about Lord Parker's justification of the *Bowman* rule is that it extends only to cases where a charity's constituent purpose is to bring about law reform. It does not extend to cases where charity advocacy is directed at other ends, such as a rethinking of government policy, or the reversal of a decision made by a government official. Another point is that the justification lacks force even in the core case of law reform at which it appears to be directed. Lord Parker might be read as saying that courts are institutionally incapable of making findings of fact about public benefit in cases where a purpose of bringing about law reform is in view. Or he might be read as saying that for constitutional reasons, courts should not make such findings of fact even if they are institutionally capable of doing so. On either reading, there are reasons to doubt that the justification offered by Lord Parker stands up to scrutiny.

Consider first the notion that courts are institutionally incapable of making findings of fact about the public benefit of law reform. Many of the cases we have looked at suggest the opposite. For example, in *Aid/Watch*, the High Court of Australia identified process benefits associated with charity advocacy, and in *Greenpeace*, *Family First* and *Better Public Media Trust*, the New Zealand courts faced factual questions about public benefit squarely, and resolved those questions in determining the cases before them. The fact that the New Zealand courts found the public benefit questions difficult to resolve does not show that the courts lacked the capability to address them, nor does the fact that judges in New Zealand have not agreed on the answers to public benefit questions in cases about political advocacy such as *Greenpeace* and *Family First*.

Now consider the idea that for constitutional reasons, courts should not make findings of fact about the public benefit of law reform. This justification seems stronger. In countries with constitutional commitments to a separation of powers in respect of the different branches of government, it might be thought that the merits and drawbacks of legislation are a matter for parliament rather than the courts. But while we might readily accept that weighing the pros and cons of legislative change, and then deciding whether or not to make that change, are matters for parliament, the separation of powers doctrine does not demand of courts that they never form views on such change. In countries like Australia, where judges administer and develop the common law, they frequently call attention to areas of social and economic life in respect of which legislative change is needed. Often, judges do this while themselves refraining from changing the common law to address the social and economic concerns in question. In taking such positions, judges are effectively stating that law reform would be of public benefit but that, for separation of powers reasons, the reform is for the parliament to take on. How, from a separation of powers perspective, does this long-established practice differ from a practice of ascertaining whether advocacy for a particular legislative change is of public benefit?

A further justification has sometimes been offered for the old *Bowman* rule. This takes the form of the argument that to find that law reform is of public benefit is to 'stultify' the law or to render the law incoherent. Again, this justification seems to extend only to cases where charities advocate for law reform rather than policy development or changes to the practices of the executive branch. And again, even in the core case of advocacy for law reform, this justification lacks force. Why would finding that law reform might benefit the public stultify the law? Why, in fact, would such a finding not recognise that law reform is needed to avoid stultification; for example, where rules of law have not kept pace with social change?

The concern about incoherence seems equally difficult to understand. In finding that a particular law reform will benefit the public, a court does not achieve the law reform in question. The court simply states a fact that is proven on the balance of probabilities in light of the evidence presented in the case. The law that stands in need of reform remains in force, and its demands are in no way contradicted or weakened. The law is no less coherent than it was before the finding of public benefit was made. In fact, it might even be argued that legal coherence is advanced where the public benefit of law reform is recognised. If a rule of law is out of alignment with underpinning policy or moral considerations, then coherence, understood now as law's conformity with policy and morality, might be served by abolishing or changing that rule. And we might press even further and question whether coherence is always a priority when contrasted with other pertinent values to which law should respond. For example, if the law could be made more coherent or more just, it seems clear enough which way the law should move. Judges, who swear an oath to do justice according to law, should not prioritise legal coherence over their primary function.

So the traditional justifications for the old *Bowman* rule are weak, and do not represent a satisfactory principled approach to the questions raised by charities and politics. Nonetheless, to the extent that those traditional justifications take an interest in the constitutional framework within which questions about charities and politics arise, they are on the right track. I now want to focus on that constitutional framework with an eye to developing an argument, not for the *Bowman* rule, but rather for a more accommodating approach to charity advocacy—one that recognises the public benefit associated with such advocacy but that also has a clear sense of the limits of that public benefit. In order to do this, we must first take a step back from the particulars of Australia's

Constitution to the liberal democratic values that animate and inspire it.

Charity advocacy is a form of political expression, and in a liberal democratic world view, political expression is a significant public good. One reason for this is the contribution that such expression makes to the individual freedom that is so highly prized within liberalism. It enables citizens to articulate and publicise their beliefs, preferences and values, testing them for plausibility and subjecting them to the scrutiny of others in public debate. This sort of critical engagement with one's own beliefs, preferences and values is an important component of a self-determining life. Moreover, political expression is a means by which ideas about politics take shape, and are revised, refined and debated. These ideas constitute pathways and options that free people can engage with in contributing to the political life of the community. In sum, then, political expression helps to generate a cultural environment in which people can live meaningfully autonomous lives as politically engaged citizens.

Political expression also plays a critical role in the maintenance of democracy. Democratic government depends on much more than an electoral system translating voting preferences into representative

government. It turns on government being responsive to citizens, not acting corruptly or with partiality,
and refraining from manipulating the preferences of
citizens. Democracy also depends on citizens being
able to disseminate, access and evaluate information
about government, its policies and its laws, so as
to hold government to account. And democracy is
enhanced by a culture in which citizens are equally
valued as members of the political community,
and where government manifests this respect by
not silencing, interfering with or even in most
circumstances disapproving of citizens' speech. These
conditions depend in important ways on a robust
culture of free political expression.

There are reasons, then, for thinking that political expression is of public benefit in light of liberal
democratic values. These reasons do not delineate
an argument that singles out charity advocacy as
especially beneficial to the public, but there are
further reasons for thinking that charities make a
special contribution to the liberal democratic values
we have been discussing. Many advocacy charities
seek to advocate on behalf of the communities that
they serve, communities that are often marginalised
and alienated in society. Think of the charities that
advocate for the poor, the disabled, refugees or other

groups that have suffered historic discrimination and exclusion. Democracy demands that government is responsive not only to the voices and needs of the powerful, but also to the voices and needs of these marginalised and alienated groups. To the extent that charity advocacy gives voice to the otherwise voiceless, and puts pressure on government to give due weight to the interests of the disadvantaged, it makes a particular and important contribution to the democratic project.

The liberal democratic argument for the public benefit of charity advocacy helps to show why the reasoning of the majority of the High Court of Australia in the *Aid/Watch* case is appealing. Recall that, in that case, the majority recognised process benefits associated with charity advocacy in light of Australia's constitutional commitment to a system of representative and responsible government. In doing so, the majority brought liberal democratic values to life, via the Constitution, in the setting of charity law. To that extent, the reasoning of the majority in *Aid/Watch* reflected a principled approach to the questions raised by charities and politics. Nonetheless, it did not exhaust such an approach, for the simple reason that it offered little guidance on the question of where to find the limits of the public benefit of charity advocacy. That question is of real practical importance, because civil society organisations that engage in political expression do not always do so in desirable ways. Perhaps the best example in recent memory is the role that associations such as the Proud Boys and the Oath Keepers played in the attack on the US Capitol on 6 January 2021. In light of what sorts of argument might we say that the political expression of Aid/Watch was of public benefit in Australia while the 6 January insurrection entailed political expression that harmed the American public?

The simple answer lies once again in liberal democratic values. Political expression that undermines democracy, or the institutions that sustain it, is not of public benefit once viewed in light of such values. Neither is political expression that is directed against liberal ideals such as the autonomy of the individual. Viewed in this light, the 6 January insurrection was plainly harmful to the American public, as it entailed the expression of a political desire to overthrow the democratic system of government enshrined in the US Constitution. Equally, from the standpoint of liberal democracy, an organisation advocating for the subordination of women in public life could not be doing something of public benefit, as it seeks to order society in ways that violate the autonomy of women. And, to draw on an example closer to home, Family First's advocacy, which entailed agitating for the withdrawal of civil rights from non-traditional families in New Zealand, could not, to that extent, be for the public benefit. On the other hand, the Better Public Media Trust had a purpose of advocating for the maintenance of a robust and independent public media sector in New Zealand, a purpose that was clearly of public benefit in light of the demands of liberal democracy.

Note that the question of the public benefit of political advocacy that undermines liberal democracy is different from the question of whether the liberal democratic state should tolerate such advocacy. A liberal democratic state might prudently tolerate a range of acts of political expression that are at odds with liberal democracy, mindful that the state will not always discern correctly when political expression is justifiably silenced, and that the risk of error warrants a cautious approach. But toleration does not in any sense presuppose a judgement of public benefit. Indeed, understood correctly, toleration presupposes precisely the opposite, in that the state has formed the view that the political expression in question will not benefit the public but nonetheless chooses not to interfere with that expression on other grounds. Thus, to return to the example of Family First, the New Zealand state, through its judiciary, has articulated the view that Family First's advocacy is not beneficial to the New Zealand public. Accordingly, Family First cannot be recognised as a charity and it cannot access the legal privileges such as income tax exemption that attend that status. Nonetheless, Family First is completely free to continue with its advocacy in the absence of state endorsement and support—as indeed it is doing according to its website.[33]

The example of Family First, and for that matter the 6 January US insurrection, suggest that the New Zealand courts have been right to insist that the public benefit question cannot be answered in respect of political advocacy without looking at benefits and detriments associated with the ends advocated for. In *Aid/Watch*, the High Court of Australia articulated the important connection between liberal democracy, the constitutional order and the process benefits of charity advocacy. However, it is also necessary to look to the ends advocated for to work out the answer to the further question of whether advocacy undermines liberal democracy notwithstanding any process benefits associated with it. And it also seems necessary to bring into view the manner in which an organisation carries out its advocacy, a further consideration to which the Supreme Court of New Zealand referred in *Greenpeace*. As we saw earlier, questions about the manner in which political advocacy is carried out were evident in *Aid/Watch* itself, where Justice Heydon in dissent thought that the strident and impatient character of Aid/Watch's advocacy was pertinent to the case.

From a liberal democratic standpoint, how should political advocacy be assessed where it is intemperate in the sense of emotive, unreasoned, uninterested in evidence and even belligerent? Trends in political culture make this question especially important for us right now. Whatever our views on the current war in Gaza, we can hardly deny that political advocacy in respect of that war has played out in Australian society in highly intemperate ways, from university encampments to attacks on private property and the offices of members of parliament, to disruptive protests at events. The style of engagement seems especially pronounced in the case of this war, but it is not limited to that issue, as the activities of environmental protest groups such as Extinction Rebellion and Just Stop Oil attest. Recently, members of the latter group sprayed orange powder paint on Stonehenge to draw attention to its demand that the UK Government outlaw extractive industries by 2030. The stunt was widely condemned, including by the druids and witches for whom Stonehenge has religious significance.[34]

Thinking through the public benefit question in respect of intemperate advocacy is not easy from a liberal democratic point of view. Within the liberal philosophical tradition, there is a line of thought that ascribes value to expression only to the extent that the expression facilitates a true understanding of the requirements of reason.[35] This rigorous view suggests that at least some intemperate advocacy lacks value as it does not invite engagement with reason. On the other hand, the famous liberal notion of a 'market-place of ideas' suggests that the discernment of truth is best enabled by the widest range of expression consistent with public safety.[36] On this laissez-faire view, intemperate advocacy might well be of public benefit even though it is confronting, emotive, and uninterested in engaging with reason and evidence. Moreover, it might be argued that some intemperate advocacy contributes to democratic government by forcing government to notice and respond to the preferences and needs of otherwise marginalised citizens in important political matters. While social and economic elites can command the attention of government in back rooms, the marginalised might have no choice, if they are to be heard, but to engage in noisy and disruptive protest.

A further set of considerations relates to the conditions under which liberal democracy can work in circumstances of moral and political diversity. What must be true if citizens who believe and care deeply about different things are to successfully maintain a shared public life built on liberal and democratic foundations? This is one of the core questions of liberal political philosophy.[37] One part of the answer to it takes an interest in the attitudes that citizens cultivate and express in their contributions to public life. This attitudinal aspect of liberalism is not often highlighted by political philosophers, but recent work by Alexandre Lefebvre has brought it very much to the fore in liberal thinking.[38] If the shared project of liberal democracy is to be sustained, it will likely depend on a sufficient number of citizens having and expressing empathy, trust and respect for others with whom they disagree deeply about moral and political questions.

This brings us back to the question of the manner in which political advocacy is carried out. Advocacy that is thoughtful, grounded in reason and evidence, and that seeks dialogue and engagement with those who disagree, is more likely than intemperate advocacy to contribute to building empathy, trust and respect. This, then, is an argument for with-holding a finding of public benefit from at least some intemperate advocacy, even where the ends advocated for might benefit the public and even though the state might tolerate that advocacy. And, by extension, it is an argument for recognising public benefit where advocacy is carried out in a way that promotes attitudes on which liberal democracy depends. Earlier, we noted a thought-provoking passage from Justice Williams's judgment in *Family First* that highlighted the importance of 'honesty and respect' in helping citizens who disagree to 'navigate ... through difficult issues'. The significance of this passage can be fully grasped once the importance of attitudes to the liberal democratic project are brought into view.

THE IMPORTANCE OF ALTRUISM

We have seen that a proper understanding of liberal democratic values brings into relief not only the argument for the public benefit of political advocacy, but also the limits of that public benefit. A further dimension of those limits remains to be explored. It was alluded to by Justice Williams in *Family First* when he made a connection between honesty and respect in debate and the 'charitable principle of self-lessness'. Here, he appeared to associate the principle of altruism that runs through the legal conception of charity on the one hand, and the value (or disvalue) of intemperate advocacy on the other.

To see how a principle of altruism animates the legal conception of charity, it is necessary to shift our attention away from the question of benefits and detriments associated with the pursuit of charitable purposes, and towards the other key element of charity law's public benefit test: the requirement that charitable purposes be sufficiently public in orientation. There is a rich seam of case law elaborating how judges and other decision-makers may distinguish between purposes that are public in the sense necessary to satisfy the public benefit test, and purposes that lack this public character.

That case law is complex and at times difficult to understand, but some principles may be extracted from it readily enough. A purpose that stands to benefit only a private class, such as members of a family or employees of a company, is usually insufficiently public to satisfy the public benefit test. In a leading decision from the 1950s, the House of Lords found that the purposes of a trust established to support the education of children of employees of

British American Tobacco was not charitable because, while the advancement of education is undoubtedly a charitable purpose type, the children of people who work for a particular company cannot be said to be a public class as understood in the public benefit test.[39] An organisation whose constituent purposes include serving the interests of its members will also usually fail to demonstrate a public character in the sense necessary to be recognised as a charity of public benefit. Thus, in a 2015 decision, Justice Digby of the Victorian Supreme Court ruled that the Law Institute of Victoria (LIV) was not a charity for the purposes of Victorian law, as its primary purpose is to look after its members.[40] The fact that the members of the LIV serve public interests through constituting a legal profession dedicated to the administration of justice and the rule of law was insufficient to lend the institute the requisite public character.

The public element of charity law's public benefit test seeks to ensure that charities are organised on an altruistic basis. It does not do this by testing for altruistic motivations on the part of those who establish charities and carry out charitable purposes. Testing for altruistic motivations in this way would be forensically challenging and an oppressive exercise of state power. Rather, the public element of the public benefit test aims to embed altruism in charitable organisations structurally. Those who wish to pursue charitable purposes must structure those purposes so that they stand to benefit people to whom special ties of affection or loyalty are not owed. Equally, charity founders must seek to benefit others without structuring their charities in a way that enables some return to themselves. Most obviously, charity founders must structure their charities on a not-for-profit basis, building into that structure non-distribution constraints that protect against the application of charity assets in the service of private interests. But the injunction against self-benefit can take other forms, as demonstrated by the case of the LIV.

What does any of this have to do with charity advocacy? The first point to note is that much charity advocacy is structurally altruistic in the way demanded by charity law. An organisation whose constituent purpose is to mount a public campaign against the detention of prisoners of conscience or in favour of nuclear disarmament seeks, all else being equal, to generate benefits that are for the public in general, as opposed to themselves or individuals or groups with whom they are associated. All else might not be equal; for example, where the campaign is to release a particular prisoner who is a family member of the charity founders. But where the purpose is oriented towards the production of public goods in the form of laws, policies and governmental practices, then the purpose is, to that extent, altruistic in the way demanded by charity law.

The point to which Justice Williams alluded in *Family First* is that all might not be equal in another sort of case as well: where an organisation has a constituent purpose of engaging in intemperate advocacy. Here, the end advocated for might stand to benefit the public. But the manner in which the advocacy is carried out might be at odds with the structural altruism that charity law insists upon. Intemperate advocacy might, to use Justice Williams's phase, have a 'self-referential' character, concerned only with propounding a viewpoint and demanding that others accept it, rather than genuinely trying to engage with others in reasoned and evidence-based ways. Advocacy with this character might be best understood as the assertion of private views rather than as a genuine effort to benefit others through political engagement. Lacking a sufficiently public character on account of the manner of its exercise, intemperate advocacy might fall foul of the public benefit test even though the ends advocated for stand to generate public benefit. Justice Williams's dicta in *Family First* point to an area for further jurisprudential development in those jurisdictions, such as Australia and New Zealand, where the *Bowman* rule has been abandoned.

Before leaving the public element of the public benefit test, it is interesting to consider the application of it to two further species of political advocacy. First, there are the constituent purposes of political parties and other partisan organisations. As we saw earlier, these purposes are not regarded as charitable in law. However, political parties seem to engage in political advocacy of exactly the sort that the High Court of Australia said was of public benefit in *Aid/Watch*. It seems clear enough that political parties advocate, in the setting of elections and more generally, for ends—the adoption of government policies—that are publicly oriented. Moreover, that advocacy is typically carried out in reasoned and evidence-based ways, even if politicians are driven to excess on that front from time to time. The constituent purposes of political parties thus seem to satisfy charity law's public benefit test and its underpinning principle of altruism. Why, then, are political parties not recognised as charities in Australian law?

It seems unlikely that an answer to that question will be found in the liberal democratic values and the principle of altruism that we have explored here. It seems more likely that drawing a clear distinction between political parties and partisan organisations on the one hand, and advocacy charities on the other, serves specific objectives relating to electoral politics as a distinct practice on which democratic government depends. This, again, is an area in need of further jurisprudential development.

In contrast stand the constituent purposes of lobby groups that aim to ensure that government is responsive to special interests. There may be some process benefits associated with these purposes. For example, lobbying might ensure that certain political viewpoints are presented to and heard by government. That said, lobbying government seems straightfor-wardly liable to corrupt political decision-making in ways that undermine and threaten democratic government. Lobbying is carried out in private, and this stands at odds with charity law's commitment to altruism as expressed in the public element of the public benefit test. In this, lobbying may be contrasted with public campaigns for law reform or policy change. Moreover, to the extent that lobbyists represent special interests—whether these be associated with a particular industry, profession, religion or identity group—their partiality is apt to lack the structural altruism that charity law's public benefit test seeks to promote.

A POLITICS OF THE COMMON GOOD

The history of charity and politics is an uneasy one. In Australia, notwithstanding the important work that charities do through political advocacy, organisations that have sought to engage in such advocacy were long denied charity status under the old *Bowman* rule. Moreover, as the background to the *Aid/Watch* case demonstrates, charities have risked losing their hard-won charity status because executive government has sought to deploy the *Bowman* rule as an instrument of control. The High Court of Australia effected a sea change in *Aid/Watch*, recognising the public benefit of charity advocacy in light of Australia's constitutional commitments. In sweeping away the *Bowman* rule, the court made it harder for executive government to interfere with charity advocacy. And the *Charities Act 2013* consolidated that more accommodating approach, at least for the purposes of federal law. Nonetheless, the post-*Aid/Watch* record makes for depressing reading, as successive federal governments have continued to reach for tools other than the *Bowman* rule with which to make life difficult for charities that speak out on issues of the day. And international comparisons show that in other jurisdictions, advocacy charities are either still subject to the *Bowman* rule or susceptible to executive overreach, or both.

This discomfiting history highlights the importance of a principled approach to ascertaining the public benefit of political advocacy, as well as the importance of identifying the limits of that public benefit. The court in *Aid/Watch*, along with the courts in England and Wales, Canada and New Zealand, point us in the direction of such an approach to the extent that they appeal to constitutional commitments. In this book, I have pursued this direction of travel, appealing to the liberal democratic values that underpin those constitutional commitments. A strong argument for recognising the process benefits associated with political advocacy can be mounted on the back of liberal democratic values, but at the same time those values demand a consideration of the ends advocated for and, in appropriate cases, a refusal to find public benefit in the case of advocacy that undermines or stands at odds with liberal democracy. And a further consideration emerges from reflection on the principle of altruism. Where an organisation has a constituent purpose of engaging in political advocacy that is not structured altruistically, it may fail the public benefit test. This may occur where the advocacy is intemperate or where it seeks to promote special interests in private.

What is needed now is further jurisprudential development to embed these considerations in charity law, so that a principled approach to charities and politics shapes and informs that body of law. This is work for the appellate courts, and ultimately the High Court of Australia, in articulating reasons for decision in key cases. Suitable cases come along only rarely, and so it is to be hoped that the courts seize opportunities when they present themselves, to ensure that charities may engage in political advocacy with a clear sense of the value and limits of that advocacy.

Further jurisprudential development will not solve all the problems or address all the questions we have covered in this book. Charities will remain vulnerable to executive governments that look for new ways to silence them and thwart their advocacy work. And some of the frontier questions that have opened up post-*Aid/Watch*—for example, about whether an advocacy charity can be a 'public benevolent institution' and thereby attract tax-deductible gifts—will not be wholly answered by the approach outlined in this book. As Ann O'Connell stated in *Equality Australia*, the meaning of 'benevolence' has to be worked out in light of a wide range of case-specific factors, and these factors go beyond the liberal democratic values that help to assess the public benefit of charity advocacy. Nonetheless, a principled approach grounded in liberal democratic values promises to inform even these frontier questions, as it enables decision-makers to take as their starting point for reasoning the proposition that political advocacy is of public benefit, and it relieves them of the burden of establishing that proposition as part of the reasoning process. Moreover, a principled approach, articulated by appellate courts in leading cases, provides charities and others with a powerful framework with which to critique and challenge efforts by the executive to interfere with charity advocacy.

I offer one further thought. There are many reasons to be pessimistic about the liberal democratic project just now. Authoritarian leaders command popular support. Vested interests exercise disproportionate influence on law and policy reform. The social and economic equality on which liberal democracy depends is rapidly receding from view as wealth, opportunities and even basic self-respect become more and more the preserve of elites. In this bleak landscape, where might we look to find resources to promote a politics of the common good characterised by trust, as opposed to a politics built around self-interest and fear? I hope this book has done enough to show that charity law contains and can develop such resources. Armed with an account of the public benefit of political advocacy grounded in and limited by liberal democratic values, coupled with its longstanding commitment to altruism as a guiding principle, charity law would have the potential to orient and encourage civil society organisations to promote the common good and foster trust within the polity. And a civil society activated in this way might help to inform and inspire political life generally. John Stuart Mill noticed many years ago that civil society can make a signal contribution to human welfare through enabling people to imagine new and better ways of living together.[41] If ever there was a time to realise that potential, it is now.

ACKNOWLEDGEMENTS

I have discussed the ideas in this book with many people over the years, and I owe each of them a great debt of gratitude. It is always risky to single people out, but I will name Murray Baird, Sue Barker, Jennifer Batrouney AM KC, Adam Parachin, James Penner and Matthew Turnour, each of whom has helped me to better understand charities and politics. Particular thanks are due to my collaborator and friend Jane Norton, whose voice and thinking is visible in much of this book, and to Marilyn Warren AC KC for her advice and encouragement in this project and so much else. Paul Smitz was a superb editor and I am deeply grateful for his significant improvements to the text. And thanks to Greg Bain for his enthusiasm and commitment to the project.

NOTES

1   For an overview of the history, see Matthew Harding,
    'Charity and Law: Past, Present and Future', *Singapore
    Journal of Legal Studies*, 2020, pp. 564–80.
2   *Bowman v Secular Society* [1917] AC 406, 442.
3   See Michael Chesterman, *Charities, Trusts and Social
    Welfare*, Weidenfeld and Nicholson, London, 1979,
    ch. 4.
4   *Molloy v Commissioner of State Revenue* [1981] 1 NZLR
    688.
5   *Royal North Shore Hospital of Sydney v Attorney-General*
    (1938) 60 CLR 396, 426.
6   James Goodman, 'Inside the Aid/Watch Case: Translating
    across Political and Legal Activism', *Cosmopolitan Civil
    Societies Journal*, vol. 3, no. 35, 2011, pp. 46, 53.
7   See *Lange v Australian Broadcasting Corporation* (1997)
    189 CLR 520, 559–60.
8   *Aid/Watch Inc v Federal Commissioner of Taxation*
    (2010) 241 CLR 539, [45].
9   Ibid.
10 Ibid, [47].
11 Ibid, [58].

12 See the discussion of James Goodman's evidence in the judgment of Heydon at ibid, [59].

13 *Aid/Watch Incorporated v Commissioner of Taxation* [2010] HCATrans 154 (15 June 2010).

14 House of Representatives Standing Committee on the Environment, *Inquiry into the Register of Environmental Organisations (Commonwealth of Australia)*, Commonwealth of Australia, Canberra, 2016, p. 90.

15 Thomas Oriti, 'Government Crackdown on Foreign Donations Could Have Catastrophic Impact, Charities Say', *ABC News*, 6 December 2017.

16 *Electoral Legislation Amendment (Political Campaigners) Act 2021*.

17 The 'governance standards' are contained in *Australian Charities and Not-for-Profits Commission Regulations 2022* (Cth), Division 45.

18 See Australian Charities and Not-for-Profits Commission, 'No Change to Governance Standard Relating to Compliance with Australian Laws', media release, 9 December 2021.

19 Andrew Leigh, *Address to the Charity Law Association of Australia and New Zealand: Global Issues in the Charity Sector*, 4 July 2024, https://ministers.treasury.gov.au/ministers/andrew-leigh-2022/speeches/address-charity-law-association-australia-and-new-zealand (viewed August 2024).

20 *Commissioner of Taxation v Hunger Project Australia* [2014] FCAFC 69.

21 Quoted at *Global Citizen Ltd v Commissioner of the Australian Charities and Not-for-Profits Commission* [2021] AATA 3313, [122].

22 Ibid, [125].

23 Ibid, [156].
24 Rachel Savage, 'Namibia High Court Overturns Law Banning Gay Sex', *The Guardian*, 21 June 2024.
25 *Human Dignity Trust v Charity Commission for England and Wales* (First Tier Tribunal (Charity)), General Regulatory Chamber, judge McKenna and member Elizabeth, 9 July 2014, [99].
26 *Human Life International v Minister of National Revenue* [1998] 3 FC 202, [13].
27 Emily Renaud, Canada Without Poverty, https://cwp-csp.ca (viewed August 2024).
28 *Canada Without Poverty v Attorney-General* [2018] ONSC 4147.
29 *Re Greenpeace of New Zealand Inc* [2014] NZSC 105, [62].
30 Ibid, [103].
31 *Attorney-General v Family First New Zealand* [2022] NZSC 80, [180].
32 *Better Public Media Trust v Attorney-General* [2023] NZCA 553, [100].
33 Family First New Zealand, https://familyfirst.org.nz (viewed August 2024).
34 Barney Davis, 'Druid Chief Condemns Just Stop Oil "Random Attention Seeking" after Stonehenge Stunt', *The Independent*, 21 June 2024.
35 See, for example, Ronald Dworkin, *Sovereign Virtue: The Theory and Practice of Equality*, Harvard University Press, Cambridge, MA, 2000, pp. 380–2.
36 The phrase 'marketplace of ideas' comes from the judgment of Justice Douglas of the United States Supreme Court in the First Amendment case of *United States v Rumely* 345 US 41 (1953), 56. But the idea is often associated with John Stuart Mill.

37 See, for example, John Rawls, *Political Liberalism*, Columbia University Press, New York, 1993.

38 See Alexandre Lefebvre, *Liberalism as a Way of Life*, Princeton University Press, Princeton, NJ, 2024.

39 *Oppenheim v Tobacco Securities Trust Co Ltd* [1951] AC 297.

40 *Law Institute of Victoria v Commissioner of State Revenue* [2015] VSC 604.

41 JS Mill, 'On Liberty', in Mill, *On Liberty and The Subjection of Women*, Wordsworth Classics, Ware, UK, 1996, pp. 73–4, 105–10. See also the account of associational life in the United States and its role in fostering a democratic culture in Alexis de Tocqueville, *Democracy in America*, trans. and ed. Harvey C Mansfield and Delba Winthrop, University of Chicago Press, Chicago, 2000.

Other books on the issues that matter:

(continued from previous page)